Leading in a Multi-Generational Workforce

Cole Herring & Brandon Sadler

Copyright © 2023 Herring & Sadler

All rights reserved.

Dedicated to those that see the vision, and have the drive to get it done.

CONTENTS

Understanding Generations	1
Baby boomers	11
Generation X	13
Millennials	15
Generation Z	17
Generation Alpha	20
Defining the Generational model of an institution	23
Baby Boomers	27
Generation X	41
Millennials	53
Generation Z	63
Generation Alpha	73
Conclusion	81

UNDERSTANDING GENERATIONS

"Understanding people certainly impacts your ability to communicate with others."
- John C. Maxwell

With five generations currently working side by side, it's more important than ever to understand the unique strengths, motivations, and communication styles of each generation. In this manual, we will explore the characteristics of each generation, from Traditionalists to Generation Alpha, and provide practical tips for effectively leading and managing people from all walks of life. Whether you're a new leader or an experienced manager, or just want to understand your teammates or boss better, you'll find valuable insights and strategies for navigating the complexities of leading a diverse team. Some early traditionalists that grew up in rural areas remember getting electricity in their household when they were kids. Contrast this with Generation Z, who's oldest members are 25 years old. They do not know life without the internet, and have no memory or were very young prior to the smart phone era. For the first time in history five different generations are in the workforce at the same time. The rapid technological advancements and change spread through these generations would be the equivalent of packing the 400 years of change following the development of the printing press in 1440, or 200 years of change during the industrial revolution from 1740-1840, into an equivalent amount of world change that spans only 80 years.

The military is structured to work with allis, and incorporate specialties across wide range of expertise that include operating on land, at sea, in the air, in cyberspace, and space. For this reason, within the military, the term "multi-domain operations" has rapidly replaced the antiquated "interoperability" as the term of choice in all things strategic competition. It is the most recent verbiage evolution used to discuss how all domains of a battlefield come together to create an effect greater than any singular domain can achieve. If we change the arena being discussed from a battlefield to an organization or a company, we can still apply the multi-domain ideology to that entity. Applied to leadership, multi-domain best describes the cross function of different generations within an organization to achieve effects that could otherwise not be accomplished. Every generation has its own unique skills and abilities, but also has challenges specific to that generation. For example, an employee born in the early 80s may be more comfortable in the middle of hostile business negotiations than an employee born in the early 2000s. That same 80s employee may also be much less comfortable in the middle of a discussion about how to modernize and increase the productivity of a computer operating system that the 2000s employee. Neither of these makes one a better asset than the other, it just requires a leader who understands the latent talents of employees from different generations and how to best utilize them.

We are all impacted by the environment we grew up in and the events that occurred as we were growing up. Some even go so far as to say that world views are created generationally. This manual is meant to provide leaders with tools that they can have as options when leading a multi-generational team, or interacting with people across multiple generations. If you are a leader with people that span across all generations, or if you are looking to understand your bosses, this guide is for you. The first step is simply understanding the generations and major environmental impacts while they were growing up that have undoubted played a role in shaping their world view.

One quick example to demonstrate the value in having cross-generational leadership tools is with communicating. We live in an era of SMS, instant messaging, colloquialisms and slang, predominantly created by millennials. When e-mail was first introduced as a substitute for sending letters, it started off with formatting as formal as those typed and handwritten notes would have been. This means it can be difficult for baby boomers to accept and adapt to the progressively informal speech surrounding today's society.

The slang and colloquialisms used by younger generations can be perceived by older generations as uneducated and an indication of lack of effort in communication. Formal communication can appear nicer to read and carries more value in terms of effort. However, it is sometimes faster and easier to use slang and abbreviations for small, less important issues, whether it's in the workplace or with family and friends. The issue with formality presents itself through digital media, rather than face-to-face communication. There are other similar pieces of knowledge throughout the book to aid equip leaders with the right tools for the right situation.

Although it helps to define the groups by year, it's important to recognize that the influences are more important. This means that an early adopter of the internet may fall more in line with traits from the millennial cohort than the latter generation x cohort. Many people also bridge between two groups. Below is a brief overview of the groups. It contains generalizations that should never be viewed as absolutes.

The modern workforce is made up of five generations of workers, each with their own unique approaches to work. Understanding these differences can help employers better manage and communicate with their multigenerational workforce.

Traditionalists, born between 1925 and 1945, are dependable and straightforward workers who are motivated by respect, recognition, and the opportunity to provide long-term value to the company. They appreciate the personal touch and prefer handwritten notes over email. Traditionalists value obedience over individualism and believe that age equals seniority. Employers can engage Traditionalists by providing satisfying work and opportunities to contribute and by emphasizing stability. Currently, they only make up

2% of the workforce, and will not have a dedicated section.

Baby Boomers, born between 1946 and 1964, are optimistic, competitive, and team-oriented workers who are motivated by company loyalty and teamwork. They value efficiency in communication and believe in paying their dues in order to achieve success. Employers can engage Baby Boomers by providing specific goals and deadlines, putting them in mentor roles, and offering coaching-style feedback.

Generation X, born between 1965 and 1980, are flexible, informal, and independent workers who are motivated by diversity, work-life balance, and their personal-professional interests. They value efficiency in communication and are resistant to change at work if it affects their personal lives. Employers can engage Generation X by giving immediate feedback, providing flexible work arrangements and work-life balance, and extending opportunities for personal development.

Millennials, born between 1981 and 2000, are competitive, civic-minded, and achievement-oriented workers who are motivated by responsibility, the quality of their manager, and unique work experiences. They prefer communication through IMs, texts, and email and value challenge, growth, and development, as well as a fun work life and work-life balance. Employers can engage millennials by getting to know them personally, managing by results, being flexible on their schedule and work assignments, and providing immediate feedback.

Generation Z, born between 2001 and 2020, are global, entrepreneurial, and progressive workers who are motivated by diversity, personalization, individuality, and creativity. They prefer communication through IMs, texts, and social media and value independence and individuality. Employers can engage Generation Z by offering opportunities to work on multiple projects at the same time, providing work-life balance, and allowing them to be self-directed and independent.

Overall, understanding the motivations, communication styles, and worldviews of each generation can help employers better engage and manage their multigenerational workforce.

Working in a multi-generational workplace can present a unique set of challenges. Each generation has its own unique work styles, communication preferences, and values. Here are some practical and useful tips to help navigate a multi-generational workplace:

Be open-minded: It's important to recognize that different generations may have different perspectives and ways of working. Keep an open mind and be willing to learn from others.

Foster communication: Encourage open communication across all generations. This can be achieved through team-building activities, group projects, or even informal get-togethers.

Provide training: Offer training and professional development opportunities to help bridge the generation gap. This can help older generations understand new technologies, while younger generations can learn from the experience and wisdom of older colleagues.

Embrace diversity: Embrace and celebrate the diversity of the multi-generational workplace. Everyone brings something unique to the table, and this can lead to creative problem-solving and innovation.

Be flexible: Be flexible with work arrangements, such as flexible work hours, telecommuting, and job sharing. This can help accommodate different work styles and preferences across generations.

Avoid stereotyping: Avoid making assumptions or stereotypes based on someone's age or generation. Recognize that individuals are unique and bring different skills and experiences to the workplace.

Encourage mentorship: Encourage inter-generational mentorship and coaching. This can help younger employees learn from older colleagues, while older employees can benefit from fresh perspectives and new ideas.

Practice active listening: Practice active listening when communicating with colleagues from different generations. Be patient, ask questions, and seek to understand their point of view.

Provide feedback: Provide feedback and recognition to all employees, regardless of their generation. This can help build a culture of respect and inclusion, while also encouraging professional growth and development.

By following these tips, you can create a more inclusive and productive multi-generational workplace. Remember, everyone has something to offer, and by working together, we can achieve great things.

BABY BOOMERS

As Baby Boomers were growing up, the economy was growing up too. This led them to be optimistic and passionate and have great negotiation skills. While every generation values respect, Baby Boomers define respect as conducting face-to-face conversations and using a deferential tone towards those in authority. A strong work ethic, to a Baby Boomer, means being on-site and in your seat.

- Born between 1946 and 1964.
- 59-77 years old (in 2023).
- 25% of current American workforce
- **Shaping events.** Vietnam war, civil rights movement, Watergate.

- **Motivation.** Company loyalty, teamwork, and duty.
- **Communication style.** Whatever is most efficient; phone calls and face to face. Perceive colloquialisms and slang predominantly established by millennials as uneducated and showing a lack of effort.
- **Worldview.** Achievement comes after paying one's dues; sacrifice for success.
- **Tips.** Provide them with specific goals and deadlines; put them in mentor roles; offer coaching style feedback.
- **Common characteristics.** Ambitions, goal-oriented, optimistic, workaholic, team oriented, and competitive. Focused and believe in more hours at work. Bureaucratic.
- Digital immigrants.
- Often careless about wealth.
- Spent a significant portion of their life communicating via a fixed line telephone.
- Although too young to fight in World War II, early baby boomers remember the events. The end of WWII created a significant amount of prosperity, and fueled a new era of consumption.

- Key historical evenest lived through include the Vietnam war, Civil Rights Act in 1964, moon landing, and cold war.
- Hippies, sexual revolution.
- TV was a key technological advancement and led to a culture of watching TV.
- In the US, African-Americans make up 10 percent and Hispanics 8 percent of this demographic group.

GENERATION X

When Generation X, or Gen Xers, were growing up globalization was just taking off. Globalization subsequently resulted in layoffs, which in turn shaped their worldview that values a need to "get things done" and efficiency. They learned to do things for themselves. Because of this, they often exhibit independence and a desire to work alone. Generation X prefer keeping red tape and meetings to minimum. Goal achievement is synonymous with work ethic.

- Born between 1965-1979.
- 44-58 years old (in 2023).

- 33% of current American workforce.
- **Shaping events.** The AIDs epidemic, the fall of the Berlin Wall, the dot-com boom.
- **Motivation.** Diversity, work-life balance, their personal-professional interests rather than the company's interests.
- **Communication style.** Whatever is most efficient. Phone calls and face to face.
- **Worldview.** Favoring diversity; quick to move on if their employer fails to meet their needs; resistant to change at work if it affects their personal lives.
- **Tips.** Give immediate feedback; provide flexible work arrangements and work-life balance; extend opportunities for personal development.
- **Common characteristics.** Independent-minded, educated, informal, casual entrepreneurial, flexible, skeptical, work hard, in debt, embrace feedback, often cynical.
- Early digital adopters.
- High divorce rates.
- Became the first to interact with technology.
- PC, surfing the internet, and using email slowing catch on.
- End of the cold war.

- Have a love of music. Generation pioneered pop culture as we know it today. Grew up watching a significant amount of TV soaps.
- Spent a significant portion of time communicating via email as they were already working age during the internet boom.

MILLENNIALS (GENERATION Y)

The oldest millennials have experienced two "once in a lifetime" economic crises during their key developmental career years. Most entered work at the height of a recession. Millennials came at the age of the internet explosion. The world was in a state of urgency when Millennials were growing up. For example, the terrorist attacks on 9/11, subsequent wars on terrorism, Y2K, school shootings, and climate change were top issues. This created a need for meaning. A company's mission statement and feeling of purpose can place considerable weight with a Millennial. They prefer collaboration and can be impatient for promotions. Millennials expect work-life integration. This means they want the ability to take off a couple of hours to handle personal affairs. To them, a strong work ethic means picking back up during the evening to complete their work.

- Born between 1980-1995
- 28-43 years old (in 2023).
- 35% of current American workforce.
- **Shaping events.** Columbine, 9/11, and the internet.
- **Motivation trend.** Responsibility, the quality of their manager, unique work experiences.
- **Communication style trend.** IMs, texts, and email.
- **Worldview.** Seeking challenge, growth, and development; a fun work life and work-life balance, likely to leave an organization if they don't like the change.
- **Tips.** Get to know them personally; manage by results; be flexible on their schedule and work assignments; provide immediate feedback.
- **Common characteristics.** Socially driven, competitive, civic and open minded,

achievement-oriented, ethnically diverse, tech-driven and curious, educated and multi-career minded, financially conscious therefore stable, poor at interpersonal skills, less religious.
- Viewed as entitled by older generations.
- Digital natives.
- Technology was taking true shape and changing productivity.
- Communicate effectively via instant messaging. Entering the workforce as smartphone started be become mainstream.
- Bore the responsibility and opportunity to fully harness technology.
- Lived through a period of rapid change.
- Known as the trophy generation for a parental style developed that gave everyone trophies for showing up. Due to this, many crave feedback while others developed a feeling of entitlement.

GENERATION Z

As children, Generation Z observed recessions and their parents had to be budget-conscious. In part because of this, they are resilient, resourceful, and realistic in not expecting their job to be a dream job. They have a can-do, self-starter attitude. Gen Z uses formalities in their dress and how they address others. They are constantly connected to devices, with positive effects in consuming information and negative effects in trends of depression and anxiety. In an era of so much content, fake content, and the filter bubble, they are quick to push through the noise. They are able to consume more information than any group before and they have become accustomed to cutting through it. They are perhaps the most brand-critical questioning group around and will call out any behavior they dislike on social media.

- Born between 1996-2009
- 14-27 years old (in 2023).
- 5% of current American workforce
- **Shaping events.** Life after 9/11, the Great Recession, access to technology from a young age.
- **Motivation trend.** Diversity, personalization, individuality, creativity.
- **Communication style trend.** IMs, texts, and social media.
- **Worldview.** Self-identify as digital device addicts; value independence and individuality, prefer to work with Millennial

managers, innovative coworkers, and new technologies.
- **Tips.** Provide work-life balance, offer opportunities to work on multiple projects at the same time; allow them to be independent and self-directed.
- **Common characteristics.** Super connected, less rebellious, more tolerant, less happy, tech-savvy, poor at interpersonal skills, reduced attention span, indoor generation, ethnically diverse, less religious, personalized learning, goal-oriented, and pragmatic.
- Drive vehicles, become sexually active, and indulge in alcoholic beverages much later in life compared to previous generations.
- Mainly children of generation X.
- Digital innates. Do not remember or know a time before the internet. Do not know or were very young before the smart phone era.
- Will make up 27% of the workforce by 2025.
- Ironically, excluding the technological aspects, experts compare their similar traits to the silent generation from the 1920s-1940s.
- More likely to hang out with parents.

- Online use and growing up with social media have created unrealistic expectations; "epidemic of anguish."
- Huge amounts of information at their disposal growing up affected their sense of concentration.
- Often have been overparented which resulted is being timid about exploration, afraid to make mistakes, and unable to advocate for themselves.

GENERATION ALPHA

Generation Alpha has not entered the work force. Information is still being collected. Below is a brief over understand the trends. Detailed information on Generation Alpha will not be covered.

- Born between 2010-2025
- Currently 6-13 (in 2023).
- Born when the iPad was being released. True digital natives.
- Immersed in touchscreen devices.
- Impacted by the COVID-19 pandemic during childhood.

- Cleaner, sleep better, and eat more nutritious meals than previous generations.
- Data is still being collected.

DEFINING THE GENERATIONAL MODEL OF AN INSTITUTION

It probably is understood but building trust and leading in a multi-generational domain all begins with understanding the generational dynamic within your organization. It is easy to simply look at the year people were born and then lump them into an age defined generation. I would argue that a better way to define a generation is by their access to technology during their formative childhood and teen years. In my personal experience, access to technology has a definitive effect on the way people communicate and process information.

It is important to realize though that time and technology are not exact across the whole of the world. If you are thinking "What on earth is this guy talking about? The first iPhone came out all over the country on June 29th, 2007" You are absolutely correct, however I said, "access to technology", not release date of technology. If you lived in an urban environment like Los Angeles and had the excess funds available, you may have had access to technology years before someone who lived on a tight budget in rural Montana. You are the same age as that person, but their access to technology may have come several years later than yours.

Like with any theory that generalizes large groups of people, there will always be a small percentage of outliers who do not fall within the generalization. I am sure you have personally met one or more of these outliers if you have any significant amount of time in a large organization. I would ask you to apply the thoughts in this book to the remaining 98% and not use the 2% to disregard it entirely.

Chronological generation definitions

PA generation or Public Arcade generation: these fossils predate even the earliest Nintendo civilization. It is highly unlikely they had a personal phone in their room, in fact, they probably remember watching the phone dial spin back around after dialing a 9. Most likely sat on the edge of their seat as JR Ewings killer was revealed.

NC or Nintendo Civilization: these day walkers are the crossover generation, they no longer had to travel to a public arcade, but were forced to sit beside each other for multi-player games. They may have had their own phone in their room, but most likely shared a single line with the entire family. They are as proficient with White-out as they are with a backspace key. Probably still remember the important codes when calling their friends pager. Most likely sat on the edge of their seats as Mr. Burns killer was revealed.

Cellular Pioneers: while not yet building urban landscapes in Minecraft, these brave souls ventured into the dangerous hinterlands of

Limewire and cell phones without cases. They still remember the satisfaction of slamming a flip phone shut when their crush broke up with them. Their teen years were defined by where they ranked on their friends top 8. Spent their teen years praying they did not go over the minutes on their plan and telling their friends to call them back after 9pm.

Internet Utopians: "give me connectivity or give me death!" in the hierarchy of technology these souls are the peak of human evolution (so far). They have friends worldwide who they may have never met, but have potentially battled alongside against a horde of orcs. Not feeling their phone when they reach into their pocket may result in the onset of a panic attack.

INSTITUTIONAL GENERATION DEFINITIONS

This is defined relative to your position in an organization and can also be broken into four groups of individuals. Your Position in the organization is used as the starting point for the separating the groups.

Your Peers: this group is comprised of people in an organization who have similar time in the organization and hold a position similar to yours in the organization.

Mentors: this group is comprised of people who are senior to you by virtue of position within the organization. Typically, this group is also senior to you in terms of time within the organization, but that is not always true as some people may have outpaced you within terms of promotion.

Near peers: this group is comprised of people in the organization who would consider you an immediate mentor. They are junior to you by virtue of position within the organization. This group is further subdivided by age, depending on their track within the organization they may be either older or younger than yourself.

Initial Entries: this group is comprised of people brand new to the organization. As a general rule, they are junior to you and are younger than you, however swings within the employment trends may on occasion violate this when older individuals enter new organizations.

DEFINING THE GENERATIONAL MODEL OF AN INSTITUTION

BABY BOOMERS

"Nobody in life gets exactly what they thought they were going to get. But if you work really hard and you're kind, amazing things will happen."
– Conan O'Brien

The population of the United States exploded after WW2 and the birthrate continued to rise at the end of the Korean War in 1954 but then slowly declined as the American involvement in the Vietnam began to increase. The 77 million babies born between 1946 and 1964 are referred to as the Baby Boomers. There were many factors that contributed to the Baby Boom, but the most important factors were the end of the Depression (1929 - 1939), the end of WW2 (1939 - 1945) and the end of the Korean War (1950 - 1953).

The years of the Baby Boomers saw the largest ever increase in the U.S. population, stimulating the post-war economies and producing a substantial rise in demand for consumer goods. The Baby Boomers represent nearly 20% of the U.S. population, and have a significant impact on the economy. Baby Boomers are an affluent group and now make up 70% of the nation's disposable income. As a result, the Baby Boomers are often the focus of advertising, marketing campaigns and financial and business planning.

Devastating wars and periods of economic recession result in a fall of the birthrate. The end of such events are greeted with a new sense of optimism in a booming postwar economy and young couples, who had delayed marriage, could now marry, buy their own homes and begin to raise their own families.

The U.S. government encouraged the growth of families by providing generous provisions for returning GIs, to make young couples feel able and willing to support children. The Servicemen's Readjustment Act of 1944, provided low-cost mortgages and low-interest loans for buying or building homes and by the end of the duration of the act in 1956, 4.3 million home loans had been guaranteed by the government. The G.I. Bill also financed a well-educated work force and the middle class swelled. By 1956, for the first time ever in the history of the United States, white-collar workers outnumbered blue-collar workers.

Between 1946 and 1956 the average income of American families nearly tripled. $200 billion in war bonds matured, and the period from the end of World War II to 1964 saw the rise in consumerism as people were increasingly influenced by advertising in magazines and television and popular culture celebrated parenthood, pregnancy and large families.

People had money to spend and the economic boom led to a rush to purchase new, inexpensive homes in the suburbs to obtain better housing and a higher standard of living. The number of

Americans buying their own homes rose form about 40% to 60%.

The parents of the Baby Boomers had suffered great levels of discomfort and uncertainty throughout their generation. As a result, they influenced the children to place a high value on security and comfort.

The Baby Boomers enjoyed a lifestyle and standard of living that had never been witnessed before. Their homes were filled with the latest appliances and luxury items and many families had enough disposable income to purchase a second car.

New, sophisticated, advertising techniques were used to tempt affluent consumers and companies employed elaborate marketing campaigns across the media to sell their brands and encourage people to develop material aspirations. The baby boomers were the first generation of American children and teenagers with significant spending power fueled the growth of massive marketing campaigns and the introduction of new, recognized branded products. Marketeers focused on the prospect of gaining a young consumer with lucrative, long-term potential.

Below are tips on leading and managing baby boomers.

1. Foster a sense of loyalty: Baby boomers value loyalty and may be more likely to stay with a company for a longer period of time if they feel a sense of loyalty and commitment to the organization. Consider creating a company culture that promotes loyalty and rewards long-term employees.

2. Provide opportunities for mentorship: Baby boomers often enjoy mentoring and coaching younger employees, and may appreciate the opportunity to share their knowledge and experience with others. Consider setting up mentorship programs or pairing older employees with younger employees for coaching and development.

3. Encourage teamwork: Baby boomers often value teamwork and collaboration, so create opportunities for your team to work together and collaborate on projects. Consider implementing team-building activities and

encouraging open communication within the team.

4. Provide a clear path for advancement: Baby boomers often value career advancement and may be motivated by the opportunity to move up within the company. Consider creating a clear career development path for your team and offering opportunities for advancement.

5. Communicate effectively: Baby boomers often prefer face-to-face communication and may not be as comfortable with newer forms of communication, such as messaging apps or social media. Make sure to communicate with your team in a way that they feel comfortable with, and consider using multiple methods of communication to reach all team members.

6. Provide ongoing support and feedback: Baby boomers may appreciate ongoing support and feedback from their leaders, so consider implementing a feedback and coaching program to provide ongoing support and development for your team.

7. Offer work-life balance: Baby boomers often value work-life balance and may appreciate the

opportunity to have a flexible work schedule or work from home. Consider offering flexible work arrangements to help your team maintain a healthy balance between their professional and personal lives.

COLLECTION OF RECOLLECTIONS ON GROWING UP AS A BABY BOOMER

All experiences growing up are different. These are simply a collection of experiences to help other generations understand differences while they were growing up. As with all of the information, they should not be viewed as absolutes. Rather, they are a mechanism for understanding different generations, which will equip leadership with tools to use for communicating with and influencing other.

Politics in the 1970s were marked by events such as Watergate and the first Presidential resignation, leading to a sense of mistrust in authority figures. In this era, our parents who grew up in the 1960s faced a dilemma of balancing setting limits and allowing freedom for their children, resulting in an ambiguous set of rules for teenagers. As a reflection of the times, science fiction stories like "Logan's Run" portrayed a future where people were required to die at a young age. The prevalence of drugs such as marijuana, cigarettes, and alcohol among teens was influenced by the drug culture left over from our parents' college days. The lack of quality TV shows resulted in everyone watching the best ones on the same night and discussing them the next day.

We were given a lot of freedom to explore the world on our own without much concern for our safety, other than warnings about the sexually transmitted disease herpes. There was an expectation that teenagers would experiment with drugs and have sex, as "Just say no" had not yet been popularized. Compared to the drug scene in the following decades, the use of prescription drugs like Valium and Ritalin, as well as drugs like pot, LSD, and cocaine, were more common among teens. Date rape drugs were either not known or not widely used. Without the internet, spreading information about such things was much slower.

We were amazed by the introduction of microwave ovens, and calling "time" on the phone to synchronize with others was a cool thing to do. We grew up with the threat of nuclear war and were aware of the nearest bomb shelter, but our local communities felt safe. Walking to school alone and playing games in the street were normal activities. Pierced ears were still a big deal and were performed in a doctor's office with much mystique.

Streaking became a bizarre practical joke among teenagers in the 70s, as there was nothing left to protest after the end of the Vietnam War. We could buy cigarettes at age 12 and beer at 14, and the consequences of being caught with drugs or alcohol were generally mild. Watching ABC, CBS, or NBC were the main TV channels, with only a few UHF stations offering old movies and cartoons. We spent most of our time outside playing sandlot games without seat belts, motorcycle helmets, or bicycle helmets.

The 1970s saw progressive sexual liberation and the advent of pornography, and education was full of experiments with new forms of teaching. Phone calls were more expensive, and the lack of answering machines and voice mail meant you had to leave a message with whoever answered the phone. Movies were only available in theaters or on over-the-air television channels, and stereo equipment was expensive and of lower quality. The absence of home video tape recorders meant catching a particular old movie on TV could take years, with lots of commercials.

In terms of fashion, the 70s were known for bell-bottoms, platform shoes, and polyester shirts with wide collars. The disco era brought in a new wave of flashy clothing, with shiny fabrics and bright colors. For women, there were jumpsuits and dresses with slits up to the thigh, while men rocked leisure suits with shiny lapels. Hairstyles were also a big deal, with long hair for men and feathered hair for women.

In the world of music, the 70s saw the rise of disco, funk, and punk rock. The Bee Gees were on top of the charts with their disco hits, while funk legends like James Brown and George Clinton were taking the genre to new heights. Meanwhile, punk rock was gaining popularity with bands like the Sex Pistols and The Clash.

One of the defining moments of the decade was the end of the Vietnam War, which had been raging since the 60s. The war had been a divisive issue in American society, with many protesting the conflict and others supporting it. The end of the war brought a sense of relief, but also a feeling of disillusionment with the government and the military.

The 70s were a time of social change and cultural upheaval. The era brought about new ideas and attitudes, and pushed the boundaries of what was considered acceptable. While some may look back on the decade with nostalgia, others may view it as a time of uncertainty and unrest.

STORY 2

As a teenager growing up in the 1970s, life was different than it is today. Technology was not yet as advanced, so our entertainment options were limited to things like records, board games, and outdoor activities. We didn't have cell phones, the internet, or social media, which meant that we had to spend more time face-to-face with our friends.

Fashion was a big part of our culture, and bell-bottoms, tie-dye, and platform shoes were all the rage. I remember spending hours putting together the perfect outfit for a school dance or a night out with friends. Music was also a big part of our lives, and we would spend hours listening to records, going to concerts, and discussing our favorite bands with friends.

In terms of social issues, the 70s were a time of change and activism. The civil rights movement and the women's movement were both in full swing, and we were acutely aware of the issues surrounding them. I remember attending protests and rallies with my friends and feeling a sense of empowerment and community as we fought for change.

School was challenging, but it was also a time of exploration and self-discovery. We were encouraged to think critically, express ourselves creatively, and develop our own unique perspectives. There was a sense of optimism and possibility in the air, and we felt like anything was possible.

BABY BOOMERS

GENERATION X

"Failure is an option here. If things are not failing, you are not innovating enough."
- Elon Musk

"Sitting there laughing at a war between Millennials and Boomers is a perfect Gen X pastime."
- J. Elvis W.

Generation X, also known as the "middle child" generation, is the demographic cohort born between the mid-1960s and the early 1980s. They are often described as being sandwiched between the more well-known Baby Boomers and the highly publicized Millennial generation.

Members of Generation X are currently between the ages of 42 and 56, and many of them came of age in the late 1970s and early 1980s as teenagers. During this time, corded phones were the primary means of communication and shopping malls were a popular destination for leisure and shopping. MTV was also a major influence on fashion and culture, setting trends for young people.

In 1983, 46% of 16-year-olds had their driver's license, which was seen as a symbol of independence and a ticket to freedom and opportunity. However, today, the percentage of 19-year-olds with a driver's license has decreased to less than 28%. This decline can be attributed to the increasing use of smart phones and other forms of communication, which have reduced the need for person-to-person contact and made it easier to coordinate rides without a driver's license.

Generation X is known for being independent and self-sufficient, with many of them coming of age during a time of economic uncertainty and social change. They are often characterized as being skeptical and distrusting of institutions, and tend to value practicality and efficiency over ideology.

In terms of technology, members of Generation X grew up with the emergence of personal computers and the internet, but were not as reliant on these technologies as the Millennial generation that followed. They also came of age during a time of significant cultural change, with the rise of punk and alternative music, and the decline of traditional gender roles and expectations.

One of the defining events of the generation was the collapse of the Soviet Union and the end of the Cold War, which had a significant impact on global politics and economics. The generation also witnessed significant advancements in science and technology, including the Human Genome Project and the expansion of the internet.

In the workplace, members of Generation X are often seen as being more collaborative and open to new ideas than their Baby Boomer predecessors. They value work-life balance and are more likely to prioritize their personal lives over their careers.

Overall, Generation X is a diverse and multifaceted generation that has had a significant impact on society and culture. Despite being often overlooked in favor of the Baby Boomers and Millennials, they have made their mark on the world and will continue to shape the future.

Below are tips on managing and leading people in generation X.

1. Offer flexibility: Generation X values work-life balance and may appreciate flexible work arrangements, such as telecommuting or flexible work schedules. Consider offering options that allow employees to better manage their personal and professional responsibilities.

2. Provide opportunities for advancement: Generation X values career advancement and may be motivated by opportunities to take on new responsibilities and challenges. Consider offering training and development opportunities, such as leadership programs or mentorship opportunities, to help employees advance in their careers.

3. Foster a sense of independence: Generation X values independence and may prefer to work autonomously rather than being micromanaged. Consider providing guidance and support, but also give employees the freedom to manage their own work and take on new challenges.
4. Provide regular feedback and support: Generation X values feedback and support from their leaders. Consider implementing a feedback and coaching program to provide ongoing support and development for your team.
5. Encourage open communication: Generation X values open and honest communication, and may appreciate opportunities to share their thoughts and ideas with their leaders. Encourage open communication and listen to your team's feedback and concerns.
6. Foster a collaborative work environment: Generation X values teamwork and collaboration, so creating a collaborative and inclusive work culture is crucial for attracting and retaining this generation. Encourage open

communication and collaboration, and create opportunities for team-building activities.
7. Emphasize stability and security: Generation X values stability and security in their careers, and may be motivated by opportunities to build long-term relationships with their employers. Consider offering competitive salaries, benefits, and job security to attract and retain top talent.

COLLECTION OF RECOLLECTIONS ON GROWING UP AS A GEN X'ER

No Web. No cell phones. No streaming video. No DVRs. Life before modern technology was a world in which you had to plan things with your friends in advance, as there was no last-minute texting or "I'm here, where are you" calls. If you didn't make the necessary arrangements, you simply missed out on seeing your friends.

Driving somewhere new required paper maps and careful planning, as well as contingency plans in case things went wrong. School work was conducted entirely from books, and research required physically going to a library and using card catalogs or microfiche and microfilm.

Calling someone on the road meant finding a pay phone and having change, as well as knowing their phone number. Paying for parking also required change for parking meters.

For those living during the Cold War, the constant threat of nuclear annihilation from the Soviet Union was a constant source of stress. In hindsight, many Russians who lived through this time have said they had no idea what Americans were so worried about.

Most transactions were conducted in cash, as credit cards were not yet widely used. Debit cards were also not yet a thing, but ATMs were becoming more common, making it easier to get cash outside of banking hours.

Watching movies meant renting VHS tapes from a local video store and finding a friend with a VCR and a large TV. All music was on vinyl or cassette tapes, and portable music was limited to as many cassette tapes as you could carry with your Walkman.

There was a lot of misinformation shared among friends, as there was no easy way to verify or correct information. Libraries were not always helpful in debunking urban legends and tall tales. Identity cards were also less strictly enforced, making it easier for underage individuals to drink. Arcades were more common and financially viable during this time.

All shopping was done in brick and mortar stores, and the mall was at the peak of its popularity. Online shopping did not yet exist, but there were options for mail-order shopping through the Sears Catalog. Long-distance calls were expensive, making it costly to stay in touch with friends who lived in other cities. As a result, people often wrote letters to keep in touch.

Photos were less plentiful, as each roll of film only had 24 or 36 exposures, and the cost of film, flash, development, and printing added up. This meant that people were less likely to take a large number of photos, and selfies were largely impractical unless using a mirror. The term "selfie" did not even exist yet.

Dating was also different, as there was no Tinder or other online dating platforms. People had to actually meet in person or through mutual friends.

Fashion during this time could also be questionable, with some trendsetting choices that are now cringe-worthy in retrospect. Many people are glad that there are no photos of their neon fabric skinny ties and other fashion missteps.

STORY 2

As a teenager in the 80s, life was very different from what it is now. There was no web, no cell phones, and no streaming video. You had to make plans with your friends in advance, and if you didn't, you missed out on seeing them. I remember having to call my friends on a landline to make plans for the weekend. We would set a time and place to meet, and if someone didn't show up, we had no way of knowing where they were.

If we were going somewhere new, we had to use paper maps and plan our route carefully. There were no GPS devices or Google Maps to help us navigate, and if we got lost, we had to rely on our instincts to find our way back. Researching for school projects meant physically going to the library and using card catalogs or microfiche and microfilm.

For me, music was everything, and I had a large collection of vinyl records and cassette tapes. Portable music was limited to as many cassettes as you could carry with your Walkman. Watching movies meant renting VHS tapes from a local video store, and finding a friend with a VCR and a large TV.

Shopping was done in brick and mortar stores, and the mall was the place to be. There was no online shopping, but we could order things from the Sears Catalog through mail-order. If we wanted to stay in touch with friends who lived in other cities, we had to write letters, as long-distance calls were expensive.

Photos were also different. Each roll of film only had 24 or 36 exposures, and the cost of film, flash, development, and printing added up. This meant that people were less likely to take a large number of photos, and selfies were largely impractical unless using a mirror.

Dating was a more personal experience, as there were no online dating platforms. You had to actually meet someone in person or through mutual friends. Fashion during this time could also be questionable, with some trendsetting choices that are now cringe-worthy in retrospect.

Looking back, life was simpler and less connected, but it also had its challenges. We had to rely on our own resourcefulness and problem-solving skills, and there was a certain thrill in exploring and discovering things on our own. I cherish those memories, and while I appreciate the convenience and connectedness that technology brings, there is something to be said for the simplicity of life before modern technology.

GENERATION X

MILLENNIALS

"The question I ask myself almost every day is am I doing the most important thing I should be doing?"
- Mark Zuckerberg

Millennials, also known as Generation Y, are the demographic cohort born between the early 1980s and the mid-to-late 1990s. They are the first generation to grow up with widespread access to the internet and digital technologies, and are often characterized as being confident, self-expressive, and open to change.

In the workplace, millennials are often seen as being more collaborative and open to new ideas than their older counterparts. They value work-life balance and are more likely to prioritize their personal lives over their careers. They also place a high value on diversity and inclusivity, and are more likely to challenge traditional power structures and hierarchies. Millennials are known for their desire for transparency and communication, and they often value collaboration and teamwork over traditional hierarchy. They are also more likely to seek out opportunities for professional development and growth.

Millennials grew up with the widespread adoption of personal computers and the internet, and have never known a world without these technologies. They are often referred to as the "digital native" generation, as they have always had access to the vast amount of information and connectivity that the internet provides.

One challenge that millennials may face in the workplace is the negative stereotypes that are often applied to them. These stereotypes, such as the idea that millennials are entitled or lack a strong work ethic, are not supported by research and can be harmful and divisive. It is important for employers to recognize and challenge these stereotypes and to instead focus on the strengths and potential of individual employees.

To succeed in the workplace, millennials should be proactive in seeking out learning and development opportunities and be open to feedback and constructive criticism. They should also be aware of the different communication styles and expectations of their colleagues and superiors, and work to build strong relationships and connections with their coworkers.

In terms of how they grew up, millennials are the first generation to have grown up with the internet and widespread access to digital technologies. This has had a significant impact on their communication, socialization, and learning habits. Many millennials have grown up with a strong sense of community and connection, thanks to social media and other online platforms.

However, millennials have also faced unique challenges, such as the rise of student debt and the impact of the Great Recession on their job prospects. Many millennials have had to navigate a rapidly changing job market and a shifting economic landscape, and have had to be adaptable and resilient in order to succeed.

Overall, millennials are a diverse and multifaceted generation that is shaping the future of the workplace and the world. It is important for employers and coworkers to recognize and respect the strengths and potential of this generation, and to work together to create a positive and inclusive work environment.

Below are tips for leading and managing Millennials.

1. Provide regular feedback: Millennials thrive on feedback, so be sure to provide frequent, specific, and constructive feedback to help them improve their work and develop their skills.

2. Create a positive work culture: Millennials value a positive work environment, so make sure your workplace is a positive, collaborative, and inclusive environment.

3. Offer opportunities for growth: Millennials are highly motivated by learning and development, so offer opportunities for

growth, training, and development to keep them engaged and motivated.
4. Be flexible: Millennials appreciate work-life balance and flexibility, so try to be flexible with scheduling, remote work, and other work arrangements to help them maintain a healthy work-life balance.
5. Embrace technology: Millennials are digital natives and highly tech-savvy, so make sure your workplace is up-to-date with the latest technology and tools to help them work more efficiently and effectively.
6. Encourage collaboration: Millennials are highly collaborative and team-oriented, so create opportunities for team projects, brainstorming sessions, and other collaborative activities to help them work together and share ideas.
7. Provide clear expectations: Millennials appreciate clear goals and expectations, so make sure you communicate your expectations and goals clearly and provide regular updates on progress and performance.

8. Celebrate achievements: Millennials value recognition and appreciation, so be sure to celebrate their achievements and successes and acknowledge their contributions to the team and the organization.
9. Be open to new ideas: Millennials are highly innovative and creative, so be open to new ideas and suggestions, and encourage them to share their ideas and opinions.
10. Foster a sense of purpose: Millennials value meaningful work that makes a difference, so help them connect their work to a larger purpose and show them how their work contributes to the success of the organization and society as a whole.

COLLECTION OF RECOLLECTIONS ON GROWING UP AS A MILLENNIAL

Being a teenager in the 2000s was a unique experience that combined the early stages of the internet and social media with the pop culture and trends of the time. For many young people, this was the era in which they were introduced to the world of computers and the internet, and they had to navigate the early dial-up internet experience with its long wait times and slow page loading.

Before the age of instant streaming, many teens spent their evenings at Blockbuster Video, browsing the aisles of entertainment options and buying overpriced candy. While Blockbuster was a popular destination for many, it eventually went out of business in 2011 as more convenient and cost-effective options like Netflix and Redbox emerged. you also had to deal with the inconvenience of technology that was not yet as advanced as it is today. For example, listening to music on a DiscMan required you to stay in one place to avoid skipping CDs, and dial-up internet took up the phone line and was slow to connect.

The 2000s were also the heyday of reality TV, and many teens communicated with their friends on nights and weekends when phone calls were free. Texting was not as widespread during this time due to limits on the number of texts that could be sent, and the fear of accidental charges for using the mobile web. Blackberries and T-Mobile Sidekicks were popular devices among teens, but they were eventually overshadowed by the iPod and Blu-Ray.

The 2000s were also the era of AOL Instant Messenger, which allowed teens to stay in touch with their friends while maintaining a sense of detachment. MySpace was also a popular social media platform, with its controversial Top 8 feature that ranked users' friendships and could cause tension among mid-level friends. Facebook, on the other hand, was initially only available to college students with a .edu email address, which added to its mystique.

STORY 2

Growing up in the late 1990s and early 2000s, I remember the excitement of the internet and the promise of an interconnected world. The sound of the dial-up modem connecting was a familiar one, and it always came with a sense of anticipation. Waiting for a webpage to load was an exercise in patience, and we often had to wait for several minutes before the page was fully loaded. However, this did not stop us from spending hours exploring the vast expanses of the World Wide Web.

One of the biggest pastimes of my teenage years was going to Blockbuster Video. There was something special about walking up and down the aisles, picking out movies, and indulging in overpriced candy. We would spend hours there, browsing through the various sections and arguing over which movie to rent. Eventually, Blockbuster went out of business, and I remember feeling sad that such a significant part of my teenage years was gone.

Technology during this era was not yet as advanced as it is today, which meant we had to deal with its inconveniences. Listening to music on a DiscMan was a big deal, but it required us to stay in one place to avoid skipping CDs. Dial-up internet took up the phone line and was slow to connect, and we often had to wait for our turn to use the computer.

Communicating with our friends was a different experience as well. Texting was not as widespread as it is today, and we were always mindful of the limited number of texts we could send before incurring additional charges. We used Blackberries and T-Mobile Sidekicks to stay connected, but these devices were eventually overshadowed by the iPod and Blu-Ray.

AOL Instant Messenger was the primary way we stayed in touch with our friends. We spent hours chatting with our friends, sharing links, and creating clever screen names. MySpace was also a popular social media platform, with its controversial Top 8 feature that often caused tension among mid-level friends. Facebook was initially only available to college students with a .edu email address, which added to its exclusivity.

Being a teenager in the late 1990s and early 2000s was a unique experience that combined the early stages of the internet and social media with the pop culture and trends of the time. Looking back, it was a simpler time, and I cherish the memories of exploring the internet with dial-up, spending time at Blockbuster Video, and staying in touch with friends through AOL Instant Messenger.

GENERATION Z

"We care about our world. We care most about the humans in our world."
- Lucie Greene

"Whenever I'm bored, I can always find something to do on my phone."
- Anonymous

Generation Z, also known as Gen Z or Gen Zers, is the demographic cohort born between the mid-to-late 1990s and the early 2010s. As the first generation to grow up with the widespread use of smartphones and social media, Gen Z is often referred to as the "digital native" generation.

Growing up as a member of Gen Z has been shaped by the rapid pace of technological change and the increasing interconnectedness of the world. From a young age, Gen Zers have been able to access a vast amount of information and connect with people from all over the world through the internet and social media.

Gen Z is also known for their social and political activism, as they have grown up during a time of significant social and political turmoil. Many Gen Zers are passionate about issues such as climate change, racial justice, and gender equality, and they are using their digital literacy and social media platforms to advocate for change.

In the workplace, Gen Z is known for their desire for flexibility and work-life balance. They value transparency and communication in the workplace, and they are often more open to new technologies and ways of working than previous generations.

One of the defining characteristics of Generation Z is their access to technology. Unlike previous generations, who may have had to rely on traditional media like TV and radio, Gen Z grew up in a world where smartphones and the internet were ubiquitous. This has both positive and negative consequences. On the one hand, Gen Z has unparalleled access to information and resources, which has helped them become more informed and engaged in social and political issues. On the other hand, technology can be a double-edged sword, with social media in particular contributing to issues like cyberbullying, social isolation, and a constant need for validation and attention.

Another defining characteristic of Gen Z is their diversity. Compared to previous generations, Gen Z is more likely to come from multicultural or blended families, and more likely to identify as part of the LGBTQ+ community. This has led to greater awareness and acceptance of different cultures, identities, and lifestyles, but also to challenges like discrimination and unequal treatment.

Finally, growing up as a teenager in Gen Z has been shaped by a number of significant social and political events, from the global financial crisis to the #MeToo movement and Black Lives Matter protests. These events have forced Gen Z to grapple with issues like economic inequality, systemic racism, and gender-based violence, and have inspired many young people to become more politically engaged and active.

Below are tips when leading someone from Gen Z.

1. Understand their needs and preferences: Generation Z is known for valuing work-life balance, diversity, and personalization in the workplace. As a leader, it's important to understand their needs and preferences, and to create an environment that supports their values.

2. Use technology to communicate: Generation Z is native to technology and digital communication, so it's important to use technology as a way to communicate with them. This could include using messaging apps, video conferencing, and other digital tools to stay connected and communicate effectively.

3. Provide opportunities for growth and development: Generation Z values growth and development, and they are often eager to learn and take on new challenges. As a leader, it's important to provide opportunities for them to grow and develop, whether through training and development programs, mentorship, or other professional development opportunities.
4. Foster a culture of inclusivity and diversity: Generation Z values diversity and inclusivity, and they are more likely to thrive in environments that embrace these values. As a leader, it's important to create a culture of inclusivity and diversity, and to encourage open communication and collaboration among team members.
5. Give them autonomy and independence: Generation Z values independence and autonomy, and they are often more productive when given the freedom to make their own decisions and solve problems on their own. As a leader, it's important to give them the space to be independent and to make decisions that support their own growth and development.

6. Stay open to feedback and new ideas: Generation Z is known for being innovative and open to new ideas, and they often have fresh perspectives on how to approach problems and challenges. As a leader, it's important to stay open to their feedback and ideas, and to encourage them to share their thoughts and suggestions.
7. Set clear goals and expectations: Generation Z values clear goals and expectations, and they are more likely to be productive and motivated when they know what is expected of them. As a leader, it's important to set clear goals and expectations, and to provide regular feedback and support to help them achieve success.

COLLECTION OF RECOLLECTIONS ON GROWING UP AS A GEN Z'ER

As a teenager, you are constantly bombarded by the distractions of the internet and social media. While you appreciate the opportunities and choices that are available to you, you also feel uncertain about your future and what path you should take.

You are busy. Your friends are busy. The second derivative of your academic workload, represented as a function of time, is permanently positive. You are amazed by the changes that are happening in the world, and you are excited by the idea of independence and being able to do whatever you want. However, you are also worried about the competitive nature of the world and whether you will be able to succeed.

Dating and romance can be confusing in the age of social media and online dating, and you may feel overwhelmed by the vast number of potential partners available to you. You are also bemused by the older generation who may struggle with technology and by those who hold outdated views on social issues such as discrimination and LGBTQ+ rights.

You may find it frustrating to memorize information that can be easily accessed online, and you may struggle to get enough sleep due to the constant demand for your attention.

STORY 2

Growing up as a teenager in Generation Z has been a unique experience for me. I was born in the mid-2000s and have been surrounded by technology my entire life. By the time I was ten years old, I had my own smartphone and spent hours scrolling through social media.

At first, I loved the constant connection and the ability to stay in touch with my friends no matter where they were. But as I got older, I began to see the darker side of social media. I saw how it could be used to bully and harass people, and how it could create unrealistic standards of beauty and success.

Despite these challenges, I'm grateful for the opportunities that technology has provided me. I use the internet to learn new skills, explore my interests, and connect with people from all over the world.

I'm also part of a diverse community. My school has students from all over the world, with different backgrounds, cultures, and religions. I enjoy learning about different perspectives and ways of life, and feel fortunate to live in a place where diversity is celebrated.

But there are still challenges. I see how discrimination and bias can impact people's lives, and I often feel powerless to make a difference. I also see the impact of climate change and the urgency of addressing environmental issues, which has led me to become more politically engaged.

Despite the challenges, I feel optimistic about the future. I see how my generation is using technology to connect with each other and to create positive change. I feel that Gen Z is more socially conscious and politically engaged than previous generations, and that we have the potential to make a real difference in the world.

As I approach adulthood, I know that I will face new challenges and opportunities. But I feel confident that the skills and experiences I have gained as a teenager in Gen Z will help me navigate the complexities of the world and make a positive impact on the world.

GENERATION Z

GENERATION ALPHA

Generation Alpha, also known as the "iGeneration," refers to individuals born after 2010 and are the first generation to be born entirely in the 21st century. Since they are not yet part of the workforce, this section should be taken as hypothetical predictions. As the children of millennials and the first generation to grow up with technology and social media as a constant presence in their lives, Generation Alpha is shaping up to be a unique generation with their own set of characteristics and traits.

One defining characteristic of Generation Alpha is their reliance on technology. From a young age, they have been exposed to a wide range of digital devices and platforms, leading to a high level of tech literacy and comfort with using technology for communication, entertainment, and learning. This reliance on technology also means that they are adept at adapting to new technologies and changes in the digital landscape.

Generation Alpha is also known for their curiosity and desire to learn. They are constantly seeking new experiences and information, and have a natural inclination towards exploration and discovery. This thirst for knowledge has led to a trend towards early education and development programs, as parents and educators seek to provide them with the best possible opportunities to learn and grow.

In terms of their values and beliefs, Generation Alpha is shaping up to be a socially conscious and compassionate generation. They are growing up in a world where issues such as climate change and social justice are at the forefront of public discourse, and many have a strong sense of social responsibility and a desire to make a positive impact in the world.

Overall, Generation Alpha is a generation that is highly connected, curious, and socially aware. They are adaptable and tech-savvy, and have a strong desire to learn and make a positive impact in the world. As they grow up and enter the workforce, it is likely that they will bring these characteristics with them, leading to a new dynamic in the workplace. Employers will need to adapt to the changing needs and preferences of this generation, and find ways to engage and motivate them in order to foster a productive and successful work environment.

One way to do this is by embracing technology and creating a digital-friendly workplace. Generation Alpha is used to having access to technology at all times, and will likely expect the same level of connectivity and convenience in their work environment. Employers should consider implementing tools and platforms that make it easy for them to communicate and collaborate with their colleagues, and provide access to the resources and information they need to be successful.

Another important aspect is providing opportunities for learning and development. Generation Alpha is driven by a desire to learn and grow, and will likely seek out opportunities to do so in their career. Employers can support this by offering training and development programs, as well as encouraging employees to take on new challenges and responsibilities that allow them to learn and grow.

In terms of values and beliefs, it is important for employers to align with the socially conscious and compassionate nature of Generation Alpha. This can mean taking a stance on social and environmental issues, and finding ways to make a positive impact in the community. It can also mean fostering a culture of inclusivity and diversity, and creating a workplace that is welcoming and supportive for all employees.

By adapting to the needs and preferences of Generation Alpha and finding ways to engage and motivate them, employers can create a productive and successful work environment that is well-suited to this unique and tech-savvy generation.

Below are tips on managing and leading people from generation Alpha.

Foster a sense of purpose: Generation Alpha values purpose and meaning in their work, so consider communicating the purpose and mission of your organization to your team and helping them understand how their work fits into the larger picture.

Encourage innovation: Generation Alpha is known for their creativity and innovative thinking, so create an environment that encourages and fosters innovation. Consider providing opportunities for your team to try new things, take risks, and think outside the box.

Foster a sense of community: Generation Alpha values community and connection, so consider creating a company culture that promotes collaboration and teamwork. Consider implementing team-building activities and promoting open communication within the team.

Offer flexible work arrangements: Generation Alpha values work-life balance and may appreciate the opportunity to have a flexible work schedule or work from home. Consider offering flexible work arrangements to help your team maintain a healthy balance between their professional and personal lives.

Encourage continuous learning: Generation Alpha values continuous learning and personal growth, so consider providing opportunities for your team to learn new skills and develop their careers. This could include training programs, mentorship opportunities, or ongoing professional development.

1. Promote diversity and inclusion: Generation Alpha values diversity and inclusion, so make sure to create a workplace that is welcoming and inclusive for all team members. Consider implementing diversity and inclusion initiatives and promoting a culture of respect and tolerance.
2. Foster a sense of purpose: Generation Alpha values purpose and meaning in their work, so consider communicating the purpose and mission of your organization to your team and

helping them understand how their work fits into the larger picture

GROWING UP IN GENERATION ALPHA

Growing up in Generation Alpha was a unique experience for me. I was born in the mid-2010s, and technology was an integral part of my life from the very beginning. By the time I was old enough to start school, I was already proficient in using smartphones, tablets, and other devices.

One of the things that made my childhood unique was the way that technology was integrated into every aspect of our lives. We used digital assistants to control our homes, and we were constantly connected to the internet, which allowed us to learn, play, and explore the world in ways that previous generations could never have imagined.

But there were also challenges that came with growing up in a world that was so heavily reliant on technology. For example, many of us struggled with screen time addiction and found it hard to disconnect from our devices. There were also concerns about the impact that technology was having on our mental health and social skills.

Despite these challenges, I felt optimistic about the future. I was part of a generation that was growing up in a world of endless possibilities. We were being taught the skills that we would need to thrive in the 21st century, such as coding, robotics, and digital design.

CONCLUSION

In conclusion, working in a multi-generational environment can bring a variety of challenges and opportunities. As the workforce becomes increasingly diverse, it is important to recognize and understand the different characteristics, values, and preferences of each generation. By doing so, employers and employees can find ways to work effectively and efficiently together, and create a successful and harmonious work environment.

One key factor to consider is the use of technology and how it can be leveraged to facilitate communication and collaboration. With each generation having a different level of familiarity and comfort with technology, it is important for employers to create a digital-friendly workplace that meets the needs of all employees. This can involve implementing tools and platforms that make it easy for employees to communicate and collaborate with their colleagues, and providing access to the resources and information they need to be successful.

Another important aspect is providing opportunities for learning and development. With each generation having different motivations and goals, it is important for employers to find ways to support and engage their employees. This can involve offering training and development programs, as well as encouraging employees to take on new challenges and responsibilities that allow them to learn and grow. Finally, it is important for employers to align with the values and beliefs of their employees, and create a culture that is welcoming and supportive for all. This can mean taking a stance on social and environmental issues, and finding ways to make a positive impact in the community. It can also involve fostering a culture of inclusivity and diversity, and creating a workplace that is welcoming and supportive for all employees.

Working in a multi-generational environment can be challenging, but it also brings the opportunity to learn and grow from the diverse perspectives and experiences of each generation. By embracing this diversity and finding ways to engage and motivate all employees, it is possible to create a dynamic and vibrant work culture that is well-suited to the challenges and opportunities of the 21st century.

CONCLUSION

ABOUT THE AUTHORS

Brandon Sadler is a native of Niceville, Florida and has served 19 years in the Special Forces Regiment, and served in multiple leadership positions where he created high performing teams. During that time, he has seen engaged leaders who fostered trust and growth, but also leaders that did not care about anything but self-promotion.

Cole Herring has 18 years of leadership experience at various levels within the US military, including leading in the Special Forces Regiment. It is his hope that this practical guide will be of value to anyone that wishes to improve their organization by understanding the multigenerational workforce. He enjoys writing and is the author of other books, to include Leadership Challenges, A Lifetime of Change, and several children's books.

Printed in Great Britain
by Amazon